CV EXCELLENCE

ROAD TO SUCCESS

ALAN KIRKHAM

TABLE OF CONTENTS

INTRODUCTION 3

CHAPTER ONE 4

    HOW TO WRITE A GOOD CV 4

    WRITE A SUCCESSFUL CV 7

CHAPTER TWO 30

    WRITE A CV: TIPS FOR 2018 (WITH EXAMPLES) 30

    10 STEPS TO A SUCCESSFUL CV 52

CONCLUSION 56

INTRODUCTION

Curriculum Vitae: an outline of a person's educational and professional history, usually prepared for job applications. Another name for a CV is a résumé. It gives you the following valuable information on how to write a perfect CV: Identify the right personal details to include. Learn what to add and what to leave out, such as whether to include your marital status or nickname. Add a personal statement. Find out what one is and how it can be used to focus a potential employer's attention on your best attributes. Know what to include in the skill section. Discover how to bring your skills to the fore and make sure you understand the difference between transferable, job-related and adaptive skills. Mention former jobs. Brush up on the best ways to present former or current employment in a way that shows you in the best light. Don't forget your qualifications. Learn what to include, how to select relevant qualifications for a particular CV and why not listing everything exhaustively is crucial. Tailor it to the application. Gain skills with writing a CV that is adapted to an individual employer or a particular sector of industry to get the best results. Keep it up to date. Find out the best ways of keeping your CV up to date so that it is ready to go at a moment's notice. It will gives you plenty of help on how to avoid the common pitfalls found in many CVs such as poor layouts, inappropriate language or simply writing too much.inlayout and content.

CHAPTER ONE

HOW TO WRITE A GOOD CV

Writing the job-getting CV is often considered a difficult task (nothing good comes easy), but with the right guidelines, you can easily create a great resume that will boldly boast of your accomplishments in your absence.

One rule you should note, however, is that there is no 'one best way' to write a CV. You can be creative about yours (it's a free world), but there are certain things that MUST be included. We have put together some suggestions that will help place your CV in the spotlight.

Generally, CVs are of two kinds – Education-based and Experience-based. The first is used when you have got no work experience (fresh graduate) or you are applying for a research role in an educational institution. The rule is that your educational/professional qualifications come first before other information. The other, experience-based, centres more on the skills you have garnered while working. Your experience should be listed from the most recent to the oldest, not forgetting to showcase your exploits. For both, put to mind that one CV may not work for all the industries, thus, you will have to adapt each CV for each industry.

Usually, a CV should contain the following information:

1. Your personal details – name, address, age (not be compulsory), phone number, email etc. Put these information in a strategic location and in legible fonts, easily noticeable by the employer and make sure the data are current. (Some job seekers can fix in email addresses that are not theirs!)

2. Education and qualifications (starting with the highest)

e.g. 2009 – University of Lagos

• B.A. History and International Relations

• Excellent diplomatic skills and versed in three foreign languages – French, Protugese and Chinese

• Graduated with a first class grade of 4.56 and won the 'Best Graduating Student' award.

3. Work experience (current first)

e.g. 2012 (present) – Iceberg Communications Limited – Marketing Executive

Iceberg Limited is Nigeria's number one market place for electrical home appliances.

- Individually increased the monthly revenue from N150 to N235 in 6 months.

- Worked with the marketing team to spread our products from Lagos to all the 6 states of the Western Nigeria within a year.

- Won the 'Salesman of the Year" award consecutively for November and December 2011.

Do remember to link your job experience with what you are applying for. It will increase the employer's preference for you.

4. Interests/Abilities

Keep this section short. As you build up on experience, this length of this section will diminish greatly. Key things to note here are:

- Avoid clichés – Scrub off words like 'Team player', 'Motivated' etc. Trust me, they will be lost among thousands others. Be creative!

- Be specific about your hobbies – Replace 'running' with 'I jog about 300 km everyday'. This shows you are very active.

- If you have demonstrated leadership skills at any time, here is the part to show it. – I was Head Girl of The Baptist Academy High School, Ikeja from 2009 to 2010. During my tenure, the school won 3 academic awards through various competitions that I actively participated in

• If you had volunteered for anything even if it's as remote as fencing in Gloucester

• Add any other interests that are relevant to the job you are interested in.

5. References

Normally two references are required: one academic (from lecturer or project supervisor) and the other from an employer (perhaps from your internship).

The lesser the pages of a CV, the greater attention it receives. As an employer, you would not want to be bothered by CVs that look like handouts. A 2-page CV is excellent. Therefore, be direct, clear and convincing. For design, use a quality A4 white/cream paper and check out for grammatical errors and misspellings. Use good font (like Times New Roman, Verdana) and normal font size is 12 with larger sizes for subheads and if asked to use write, makes lettering legible such that an employer does not need to squint.

WRITE A SUCCESSFUL CV

A CV is a marketing document in which you are marketing something: yourself! You need to "sell" your skills, abilities, qualifications and experience to employers. It can be used to make multiple applications to employers in a specific career area. For this reason, many large graduate recruiters will not accept CVs and instead use their own application form.

An application form is designed to bring out the essential information and personal qualities that the employer requires and does not allow you to gloss over your weaker points as a CV does. In addition, the time needed to fill out these forms is seen as a reflection of your commitment to the career.

There is no "one best way" to construct a CV; it is your document and can be structured as you wish within the basic framework below. It can be on paper or on-line or even on a T-shirt (a gimmicky approach that might work for "creative" jobs but not generally advised!).

When should a CV be used?

When an employer asks for applications to be received in this format.

When an employer simply states "apply to ..." without specifying the format.

When making speculative applications (when writing to an employer who has not advertised a vacancy but who you hope may have one).

What information should a CV include?

What are the most important aspects of CV that you look for?

Personal details

Normally these would be your name, address, date of birth (although with age discrimination laws now in force this isn't essential), telephone number and email.

British CVs don't usually include a photograph unless you are an actor. In European countries such as France, Belgium and Germany it's common for CVs to include a passport-sized photograph in the top right-hand corner whereas in the UK and the USA photographs are frowned upon as this may contravene equal opportunity legislation - a photograph makes it easier to reject a candidate on grounds of ethnicity, sex or age. If you do include a photograph it should be a head and shoulders shot, you should be dressed suitably and smiling: it's not for a passport! See our Work Abroad page for more about international CVs.

Education and qualifications

Your degree subject and university, plus A levels and GCSEs or equivalents. Mention grades unless poor!

Work experience

Use action words such as developed, planned and organised.

Even work in a shop, bar or restaurant will involve working in a team, providing a quality service to customers, and dealing tactfully with complaints. Don't mention the routine, non-people tasks (cleaning the tables) unless you are applying for a casual summer job in a restaurant or similar.

Try to relate the skills to the job. A finance job will involve numeracy, analytical and problem solving skills so focus on these whereas for a marketing role you would place a bit more emphasis on persuading and negotiating skills.

All of my work experiences have involved working within a team-based culture. This involved planning, organisation, coordination and commitment e.g., in retail, this ensured daily sales targets were met, a fair distribution of tasks and effective communication amongst all staff members.

Interests and achievements

Keep this section short and to the point. As you grow older, your employment record will take precedence and interests will typically diminish greatly in length and importance.

Bullets can be used to separate interests into different types: sporting, creative etc.

Don't use the old boring cliches here: "socialising with friends".

Don't put many passive, solitary hobbies (reading, watching TV, stamp collecting) or you may be perceived as lacking people skills. If you do put these, then say what you read or watch: "I particularly enjoy Dickens, for the vivid insights you get into life in Victorian times".

Show a range of interests to avoid coming across as narrow: if everything centres around sport they may wonder if you could hold a conversation with a client who wasn't interested in sport.

Hobbies that are a little out of the ordinary can help you to stand out from the crowd: skydiving or mountaineering can show a sense of wanting to stretch yourself and an ability to rely on yourself in demanding situations

Any interests relevant to the job are worth mentioning: current affairs if you wish to be a journalist; a fantasy share portfolio such as Bullbearings if you want to work in finance.

Any evidence of leadership is important to mention: captain or coach of a sports team, course representative, chair of a student society, scout leader: "As captain of the school cricket team, I had to set a positive example, motivate and coach players and think on my feet when making bowling and field position changes, often in tense situations"

Anything showing evidence of employability skills such as team working, organising, planning, persuading, negotiating etc.

Skills

The usual ones to mention are languages (good conversational French, basic Spanish), computing (e.g. "good working knowledge of MS Access and Excel, plus basic web page design skills" and driving ("full current clean driving licence").

If you are a mature candidate or have lots of relevant skills to offer, a skills-based CV may work for you

References

Many employers don't check references at the application stage so unless the vacancy specifically requests referees it's fine to omit this section completely if you are running short of space or to say "References are available on request."

Normally two referees are sufficient: one academic (perhaps your tutor or a project supervisor) and one from an employer (perhaps your last part-time or summer job). See our page on Choosing and Using Referees for more help with this.

The order and the emphasis will depend on what you are applying for and what you have to offer. For example, the example media CV lists the candidate's relevant work experience first.

If you are applying for more than one type of work, you should have a different CV tailored to each career area, highlighting different aspects of your skills and experience.

A personal profile at the start of the CV can work for jobs in competitive industries such as the media or advertising, to help you to stand out from the crowd. If used, it needs to be original and well written. Don't just use the usual hackneyed expressions: "I am an excellent communicator who works well in a team...... "

You will also need a Covering Letter to accompany your CV.

What makes a good CV?

There is no single "correct" way to write and present a CV but the following general rules apply:

It is targeted on the specific job or career area for which you are applying and brings out the relevant skills you have to offer

It is carefully and clearly laid out: logically ordered, easy to read and not cramped

It is informative but concise

It is accurate in content, spelling and grammar. If you mention attention to detail as a skill, make sure your spelling and grammar is perfect!

If your CV is written backwards on pink polka dot paper and it gets you regular interviews, it's a good CV! The bottom line is that if it's producing results don't change it too much but if it's not, keep changing it until it does.

If it's not working, ask people to look at it and suggest changes. Having said this, if you use the example CVs in these pages as a starting point, you are unlikely to go far wrong.

What mistakes do candidates make on their CV?

One survey of employers found the following mistakes were most common.

Spelling and grammar 56% of employers found this

Not tailored to the job 21%

Length not right & poor work history 16%

Poor format and no use of bullets 11%

No accomplishments 9%

Contact & email problems 8%

Objective/profile was too vague 5%

Lying 2%

Having a photo 1%

Choose a sensible email address!

One survey found that 76% of CVs with unprofessional email addresses are ignored. Here are some (modified) graduate email addresses that you should NOT emulate!

    death_metal_kitty@hotmilk.com

    demented_bovine@gnumail.com

    so_kiss_me@hotmilk.com

    platypus_mcdandruff@gnumail.com

    busty-beth@gnumail.com

    flockynockyhillipilification@gnumail.com

    virgin_on_the_ridiculous@hotmilk.com

    yourmywifenowgraham@gnumail.com

    original_madcow_jane@gnumail.com

    circle-of-despair@gnumail.com

    rage_against_the_trolley_fish@mail.com

    sexylikewoaaaah@hotmilk.com

Others 3% (listing all memberships, listing personal hobbies, using abbreviations)

How long should a CV be?

There are no absolute rules but, in general, a new graduate's CV should cover no more than two sides of A4 paper. In a survey of American employers 35% preferred a one page CV and 19% a two page CV with the others saying it depends upon the position. CVs in the US tend to be shorter than in the UK, whereas the 2 page CV still dominates for graduates, but I do see a trend now towards one page CVs: as employers are getting more and more CVs, they tend not to have the time to read long documents!

If you can summarise your career history comfortably on a single side, this is fine and has advantages when you are making speculative applications and need to put yourself across concisely. However, you should not leave out important items, or crowd your text too closely together in order to fit it onto that single side. Academic and technical CVs may be much longer: up to 4 or 5 sides.

How do I get my CV down to two pages from three?

First change your margins in MS Word to Page Layout / Margins/ Narrow - this will set your margins to 1.27 cm which are big enough not to look cramped, but give you extra space. See www.kent.ac.uk/careers/cv/word-cv.htm#margins for how to do this.

Secondly change your body font to Lucida Sans in 10 pts size. Lucida Sans is a modern font which has been designed for clarity on a computer screen. For more on fonts see here A good rule of thumb is to have your name in about 18 points, your subheadings such as education and work experience in 14 points and your body font as 10 points.

Use tables with two or three columns for your academic results and references. See a CV using tables for modules and references here and an explanation of how to do this here.

Use bullets for content, rather than long paragraphs of text. (See the box to the right)

Finally, set line spacings to single space

If after all these tricks you are still on three pages you have to be ruthless with your content: read every single word and remove it if it doesn't add value to your CV!

The one page lean and mean CV!

In certain sectors such as investment banking, management consultancy and top law firms, a one page, highly focused, highly objective CV, now seems to be preferred. All of these areas have in common that they are highly competitive to enter and it may be that selectors, faced with so many CVs to work through prefer a shorter CV.

There is no point putting lots of detailed information into a CV which doesn't add any value, and in fact, just dilutes the impact. This is called the presenter's paradox. These CVs normally have lots of single line bullets and no personal statement at the beginning. They are full of factual, as opposed to subjective, content. You must make every word count. They focus on achievements, initiative and responsibilities more than on tasks and duties. When carefully designed, these can be the very best CVs, but also the hardest to write!

See our page on Zen and the art of CV writing for more about this.

Tips on presentation

Your CV should be carefully and clearly laid out - not too cramped but not with large empty spaces either. Use bold and italic typefaces for headings and important information.

Never back a CV - each page should be on a separate sheet of paper. It's a good idea to put your name in the footer area so that it appears on each sheet.

Be concise: a CV is an appetiser and should not give the reader indigestion. Don't feel that you have to list every exam you have ever taken, or every activity you have ever been involved in - consider which are the most relevant and/or impressive. The best CVs tend to be fairly economical with words, selecting the most important information and leaving a little something for the interview: they are an appetiser rather than the main course. Good business communications tend to be short and to the point, focusing on key facts and your CV should to some extent emulate this. The longer and more dense your CV is, the harder it is for an employer to comprehend your achievements.

Be positive - put yourself over confidently and highlight your strong points. For example, when listing your A-levels, put your highest grade first.

Be honest: although a CV does allow you to omit details (such as exam resits) which you would prefer the employer not to know about, you should never give inaccurate or misleading information. CVs are not legal documents and you can't be held liable for anything within, but if a recruiter picks up a suggestion of falsehoods you will be rapidly rejected. An application form which you have signed to confirm that the contents are true is however a legal document and forms part of your contract of employment if you are recruited.

The sweet spot of a CV is the area selectors tend to pay most attention to: this is typically around the upper middle of the first page, so make sure that this area contains essential information.

If you are posting your CV, don't fold it - put it in a full-size A4 envelope so that it doesn't arrive creased.

Research by forum3 (recruitment and volunteering for the not-for-profit sector) suggested:

Graduates sent out 25 letters per interview gained.

The average graduate will send out about 70 CVs when looking for their first graduate job. Of these, the average number of responses will be 7 including 3 to 4 polite rejections and the remainder inviting the graduate to interview or further contact.

There was a direct link between the number of CVs sent out and the number of interviews gained: the more CVs you send out the more interviews you will get.

Applicants who included a covering letter with their CV were 10% more likely to get a reply.

60% of CVs are mailed to the wrong person: usually the managing director. Applicants who addressed their application to the correct named person were 15% more likely to get a letter of acknowledgement and 5% more likely to get an interview.

Applicants sending CVs and letters without spelling mistakes are 61% more likely to get a reply and 26% more likely to get an interview. "In the age of the spell checker, there is no excuse for spelling mistakes". The most common mistakes to not show up in a spell check were: fro instead of for, grate instead of great, liased instead of liaised and stationary instead of stationery.

Set your spell checker to UK English (assuming you are British) or you will get center

instead of centre, and color instead of colour.

Other turnoffs include:

misspelling the name of the company or the addressee;

not having a reply address on the CV;

trying to be amusing;

Using lower case i for the personal pronoun: "i have excellent attention to detail".

Fonts

TIMES NEW ROMAN is the standard windows "serif" font. A safe bet - law firms seem to like it but it isn't easy to read on the screen, especially in the small font size you may need to use to get your CV on one or two pages. If you do prefer to use a serif font, try CAMBRIA which has been designed for screen readability. See the example fonts to the right to see how much clearer Cambria looks than Times New Roman.

I personally prefer sans fonts - sans fonts don't have the curly bits (called serifs) on letters. ARIAL is a standard Windows "sans" font and is now used by the BBC web site which used to use Verdana. As you can see sans fonts are cleaner and more modern than Times or Cambria and also look larger in the same "point" size (the point size is simply how big the letters are on the page). However Arial and Times New Roman are so common that they're a little boring to the eye.

Classier choices might be VERDANA or LUCIDA SANS which have wider letters than most fonts but, if you are running out of space, then Arial is more space saving, as is TAHOMA which is a narrower version of Verdana. Notice how, in the example to the right, Verdana looks bigger and easier to read than Times New Roman. CALIBRI is now the standard MS Word font but is smaller and perhaps less clear than Arial, Verdana or Lucida Sans (see the examples to the right again). Never use COMIC SANS of course!

FONT SIZE is normally 12 points for the normal font with larger sizes for subheadings and headings.

Or 10 points. My favourite CV body text font is 10 point Verdana or Lucida Sans with 12 or 14 points for sub headings.

 14 points is too big for the normal body font - wastes space and looks crude.

and 8 or 9 points too small to be easily readable by everyone, especially in Times New Roman which should not be used in sizes less than 11 points

Although many people use 12 points, some research on this suggested that smaller point size CVs (within reason) were perceived as more intellectual!

Most CVs are now read on screen rather than on paper. It's no coincidence that Serif fonts are rarely used on the web - they are much less readable on screen (Times Roman was first used on Trajan's column, 2,000 years ago!), and some fonts, such as Verdana, were designed with screen readability in mind. This web site is set in Verdana which, as you can see, is clear and easy to read.

Using bold for job titles and schools

It's a good idea to use the "bold" style for job titles and employer names in your work experience and education to make these stand out. E.g.

2003-2010 St. Paul's Girls' School, London

A-levels: Chemistry B, Biology A, Maths C

Summer 2011 Next Retail (Sales Assistant)

The job entailed working in the busy sale, taking deliveries, stock control and dealing with customers with high quality customer care.

In a survey of American employers

33% preferred the use of bold on job titles in the candidate's work history

7% preferred the use of bold on employer names from candidate work history

31% preferred bold on both

29% had no preference

Different Types of CV

Chronological - outlining your career history in date order, normally beginning with the most recent items (reverse chronological). This is the "conventional" approach and the easiest to prepare. It is detailed, comprehensive and biographical and usually works well for "traditional" students with a good all-round mixture of education and work experience. Mature students, however, may not benefit from this approach, which does emphasise your age, any career breaks and work experience which has little surface relevance to the posts you are applying for now. See an example chronological CV here

Skills-based: highly-focused CVs which relate your skills and abilities to a specific job or career area by highlighting these skills and your major achievements. The factual, chronological details of your education and work history are subordinate. These work well for mature graduates and for anybody whose degree subject and work experience is not directly relevant to their application. Skills-based CVs should be closely targeted to a specific job.

A survey of US employers found that:

49% preferred a traditional reverse chronological CV (all jobs listed in reverse chrological order including duties)

6% preferred a skills-based CV with skills related to the job highlighted

39% liked a combination of both the above styles

2% liked a portfolio with examples of completed projects

4% had no preference.

If you are applying for posts outside the UK, remember that employers in other countries are likely to have different expectations of what a CV should include and how it should be laid out. The "Global Resume and CV Handbook" (available from Reception) will help you prepare CVs for overseas employment. See our work abroad page.

Targeting your CV

If your CV is to be sent to an individual employer which has requested applications in this format, you should research the organisation and the position carefully.

In the present competitive job market, untargeted CVs tend to lose out to those that have been written with a particular role in mind. For example a marketing CV will be very different from a teaching CV. The marketing CV will focus on persuading, negotiating and similar skills where as the teaching CV will focus more on presenting and listening skills and evidence for these.

If your CV is to be used for speculative applications, it is still important to target it - at the very least, on the general career area in which you want to work. Use our I Want to Work in .... pages and sites such as www.prospects.ac.uk to get an idea of what the work involves and what skills and personal qualities are needed to do it successfully. This will enable you to tailor the CV to the work and to bring out your own relevant experience.

Even if you are using the same CV for a number of employers, you should personalise the covering letter - e.g. by putting in a paragraph on why you want to work for that organisation.

For example CVs, application forms and covering letters see www.kent.ac.uk/careers/cv/cvexamples.htm with notes highlighting points relating to the content and style.

Emailed CVs and Web CVs

Put your covering letter as the body of your email. It's wise to format it as plain text as then it can be read by any email reader.

Emails are not as easy to read as letters. Stick to simple text with short paragraphs and plenty of spacing. Break messages into points and make each one a new paragraph with a full line gap between paragraphs. DON'T "SHOUT": WRITE IN UPPER CASE!

Your CV is then sent as an attachment. Say you'll send a printed CV if required.

In which format should you send your CV?

A survey of American recruiters found that:

    63% preferred MS Office Word format .docx

    36% preferred Adobe Acrobat format .pdf

    1% preferred rich-text format .rtf

0% preferred text format .txt

0% preferred web page format .html

"Misunderstandings occur frequently via written communication. In fact, 68 per cent of employees said the emails they receive are sometimes difficult to decipher, whether it be a misinterpreted tone or rushed explanations."

The most common mistakes made via email include:

Accidentally clicking send before the email is ready;

Embarrassing spelling and grammar mistakes;

Accidentally sending a kiss at the end of a message;

Copying a client into an internal email about them;

Forwarding an inappropriate email trail;

Forgetting an attachment; and

Forgetting to blind copy (BCC) on an email (see the example above!)

PDF (portable document format) is perhaps becoming a widely used format now. There are PDF-readers for all platforms (Windows, MacOS, Linux). This also guarantees that you can be confident that it will look as you intended, no matter what reader is used to view the document and it is also secure. Modern versions of Microsoft Word contain a PDF export function or you can download a free pdf converter such as Cute pdf: you install it and then "print" the document to a folder on your PC. PDFs can however sometimes prevent keyword-scanning software on job boards or applicant-tracking systems from picking up information that allows you to be found.

You can also use MS Word (.docx) format. .docx files may not always open on computers using Linux and Apple platforms. .docx files may also contain sensitive information such as previous versions of a document perhaps leading to embarrassment. MS Word documents can contain macro viruses, so a few employers may not open these.

Some employers, though, may prefer Word as they can edit it, e.g. to add notes to refer to at interview. There is the possible problem that Word formatting can sometimes change on different computers so it is a good idea to email your CV to a friend to check that it comes out OK before sending it to employers.

There is no one "best" format as there are so many types and versions of software that you cannot always be certain that the recipient will be able to open your CV without any problems, especially if it has been produced on a PC and is being read on a Mac, or vice versa.

It is also fine to attach your CV in both Word and PDF and allow the employers to choose which they prefer!

Rich Text Format (.rtf), or html (web page format) are other alternatives but, as can be seen from the above survey, are not usually preferred.

If in doubt send your CV in several formats. Email it back to yourself first to check it, as line lengths may be changed by your email reader.

Web CVs and Electronically Scanned CVs

Web CVs use HTML format. You can include the web address in an email or letter to an employer. They have the advantage that you can easily use graphics, colour, hyperlinks and even sound, animation and video. The basic rules still apply however - make it look professional. They can be very effective if you are going for multimedia, web design or computer games jobs where they can demonstrate your technical skills along with your portfolio.

Electronically scanned CVs have been used by Ford Motors and others. Resumix is one package used for this: it has artificial intelligence which reads the text and extracts important information such as work, education, skills. For more information on this, see our page on on-line applications

LinkedIn

It's a good idea to have your profile and CV (without personal details such as your address of course: see right) on LinkedIn. In 2011, 89% of businesses planned to use social networks for recruitment and LinkedIn was by far the most popular one for this purpose with 86% of companies wishing to use it, 60% were considering Facebook and 50% Twitter. Make sure that your Facebook page doesn't carry evidence of any of your indiscretions that employers might view - making your page private and viewable only by friends and family is wise!

If you reply to a job advert, be careful about what information you give.

The following are not needed by employers but can lead to identity theft. Don't include:

- Date of birth
- Place of birth
- Marital status

Copies of birth certificate/passport documents or details of your bank.

You only need to give your first and last names, not your middle name.

CHAPTER TWO

WRITE A CV: TIPS FOR 2018 (WITH EXAMPLES)

This guide will show you how to write a great CV that's ready for 2018 and beyond.

A CV is required when applying for a job. In addition to your CV, employers may also require a cover letter and a completed application form.

What to include in your CV in 2018

While the structure of a CV is flexible, bending to your unique skill set and experiences, there are particular sections that employers expect to see on your CV regardless.

Here are the sections you must include in your CV:

Name, professional title and contact details

The first part of your CV, positioned at the top of the page, should contain your name, professional title and contact details. Under no circumstances should you title your CV with 'curriculum vitae' or 'CV' as it's a waste of valuable space. Treat your name as the title instead.

When it comes to your contact details, your email address and phone number(s) are essential. Once upon a time, it was customary to include your full address on your CV. Today, you simply need to list your town and county.

If you like, you can also include a link to your LinkedIn profile in this section – but only if it's up to date!

Personal profile

A personal profile, also known as a personal statement, career objective and professional profile, is one of the most important aspects of your CV. It's a short paragraph that sits just underneath your name and contact details giving prospective employers an overview of who you are and what you're all about.

You should tailor your profile to every job you apply for, highlighting specific qualities that match you to the role. Aim to keep your personal statement short and sweet, and no longer than a few sentences. To make the most of this section, you should try to address the following:

- Who are you?
- What can you offer the company?
- What are your career goals?

Experience and employment history

Your employment history section gives you a chance to outline your previous jobs, internships and work experience.

List your experience in reverse chronological order as your recent role is the most relevant to the employer.

When listing each position of employment, state your job title, the employer, the dates you worked and a line that summarises the role. Then bullet point your key responsibilities, skills and achievements, and bolster each point with powerful verbs and figures to support each claim and showcase your impact.

It helps to choose the duties most relevant to the job you're applying for, especially if it's a long list. If you have many years' worth of experience, you can reduce the detail of old or irrelevant roles. If you have positions from more than 10 years' ago, you can delete them.

Education and qualifications

Like your experience section, your education should be listed in reverse chronological order. Include the name of the institutions and the dates you were there, followed by the qualifications and grades you achieved.

If you have recently left education, you may write your degree, A-levels or GCSEs (or equivalents)

If you have a degree, you could list a few of the most relevant modules, assignments or projects underneath.

For professionals that are a little further along in their careers, or have many certificates in their repertoire, you can lay your qualifications out in this way:

   Qualification, grade – Institution – Year

Additional sections

There is a range of additional sections that may strengthen your CV and highlight your skills. Here are just a few you can include if you have room:

Key skills: If you're writing a functional CV, or have some abilities you want to show off to the employer immediately, insert a key skills section underneath your personal profile. You should aim to detail four to five abilities at most.

Hobbies and interests: If you feel that your CV is lacking, you can boost your document by inserting a hobbies and interests section at the end. Be careful though; avoid listing hobbies that don't add value to your CV or are run-of-the-mill, like reading. Draw on interests that make you stand out or are relevant to the job.

References: Like including an address on your CV, adding your referees to the end of your CV is no longer standardised. You can include a line that reads 'references available on request', but if you don't have room, it's acceptable to remove it altogether.

Formatting and spacing guidelines

If you're unsure of how to format your CV, it's worth downloading a few CV templates to familiarise yourself. After all, formatting and spacing your CV is equally as important as the content.

Here are some formatting and spacing tips to bear in mind:

Length: The standard length of a CV in the UK is two pages. However, one size doesn't fit all, and so for some professionals, one or three pages may be more appropriate.

Headings: Each section must be introduced by a big, bold heading to ensure an easy read.

Font type: Most employers will receive your CV in a digital format, so choose a clear font like Calibri or Arial. You can use a different font type for your headings, but keep it professional and easy-to-read too.

Font size and page margins: The body of your CV should be between 10 and 12 point font, and your headings between 14 and 18 points. Keep your page margins around 2.5cm, but never reduce them to less than 1.27cm or your CV will appear cluttered and hard to read. White space ensures clarity and professionalism.

Proofreading and consistency: Your formatting must be consistent throughout your CV to keep it looking slick. Don't spoil your polished look by including typos and inaccuracies; proofread like a pro to capture every mistake or invest in intelligent spellcheckers like Grammarly.

Tailoring, keywords and ATSs: It's perfectly acceptable to keep a generic copy of your CV for your own records, but if you're applying for a job, it must be tailored to the role. Not only will this show employers why you're a match, but it will help your application beat the ATS robots too.

Saving the file: It's likely you'll send your CV via email or through a job board like CV-Library. Save your CV as a pdf file to ensure recruiters can open it on any device. A pdf will also maintain formatting, so you can be sure that employers will see your CV as you intended.

What not to include

There are a variety of details that should not be included on your CV. Here are a few of the common ones:

A headshot: In many countries, it's common practice to include a photo of yourself on your CV. But the UK is not one of them.

Age and date of birth: The only dates that should be on your CV are from employment and your qualifications. Your age doesn't affect your ability to do the job, and it's illegal for employers to ask about age under the Equality Act 2010.

Marital status: Like your age, your marital status and dependents don't affect your ability to do your job. These details are protected characteristics under the Equality Act 2010, and it's against the law for employers to ask about them, so don't include them on your CV.

Next steps

Get your CV right from the outset, and you may well find a job more quickly. Your CV is your chance to make a great first impression and secure yourself an interview, so follow this 2018 guide and then upload your CV to apply for your next job.

EXAMPLE OF EFFECTIVE CV

When it comes to writing a CV, it helps to have a solid example of a good CV to benchmark your own CV against.

So I've put together a selection of effective professional CVs that have been used to win job interviews for our customers in the past.

Is this an effective Admin & Business Support CV?

Admin and business support staff are employed to carry out tasks that support organisations to function and can involve a range of skills from database management and reporting, to diary management and call handling.

A successful admin/business support CV (curriculum vitae) should show how the candidate supports senior figures in the organisation to deliver their services.

1. The profile gives a clear high-level explanation of the candidate's experience including the industries she has worked in and the seniority of the people she supports.

It also summarises the most important tasks that she covers in her roles - such as internal communications and professional documentation.

2. The core skills highlight important business support duties that employers will be looking for, such as typing at speed, diary management and call handling.

These bullet points jump out at the reader upon opening the CV - instantly showing the candidate's suitability.

3. Role descriptions start with a brief outline that tells readers what the employer does, who the candidates supports within the business and they type of work being supported.

Bullet pointed responsibilities go on to describe regular activities such as arranging internal events, recording client data and travel arrangement - and also show how these actions help managers and the business as a whole.

4. Older roles are squeezed down to short summaries in order to keep the CV short whilst giving employers just enough information to see the candidate's background.

5. Education is kept brief and highlights the qualifications that are important to hiring managers in the business support field, such as Secretarial Diploma and Advanced Legal Communications.

A simple format and font is used throughout the CV to create a pleasant reading experience for recruiters and employers.

Is this an effective Customer Service CV?

Customer service staff act as the "face" of their employer; ensuring that customers are looked after whilst also acting in the best interest of the business.

Your customer service CV should show employers that you are professional yet friendly, with a sound knowledge of the industry you operate in.

1. The profile gives a clear indication of the types of businesses that the candidate has worked in; shows how they interact with customers in their roles and the services they are familiar with providing.

2. The core skills highlight important customer services skills that employers will be searching for such as complaint handling and transaction processing.

This candidate also highlights their language skills because being multilingual could be very useful in a customer facing role.

3. Role descriptions start with a brief description of the employers service and explain how the candidate interacts with customers to help provide these services

Bullet pointed responsibilities explain day-to-day activities and how each one helps customers and supports the employers goals.

A good key achievement has been added which quantifies the candidate's value by showing the percentage of complaints that have been resolved within a targeted time. You can also check out our sales assistant example CV for an example of somebody working within a retail store, our customer service CV guide, or even our waiter/waitress CV example. We also have an example nursing CV.

Is this an effective Education CV?

CVs for educators such as teachers and lecturers need to project the candidate's expert subject knowledge whilst also demonstrating their abilities to educate their students successfully and work collaboratively with other staff members.

1. The profile provides an overview of all the key information that an education institution needs to know such as;

Age of students worked with

Type of institution worked in School/University/College etc.

Subjects and Curriculum taught

Number of students worked with

2. The core skills highlight important skills that a primary school would look for in this case, like behaviour management, classroom preparation and SEN support

These bullet points jump out at the reader upon opening the CV - instantly showing the candidate's suitability for teaching assistant roles.

3. Role descriptions start with a brief description of the education institution, the type of curriculum being taught and who the candidate reports to and supports.

Bullet pointed responsibilities explain day-to-day activities and how each one helps to educate students as well as support the functioning of the school.

Older and less relevant roles at the bottom of the CV are shortened to list format, in order to save space and ensure readers focus on earlier roles.

Is this an effective Finance & Accounting CV?

A strong accounting or finance CV should demonstrate the candidate's ability to manage an organisation's financial affairs by detailing their qualifications, knowledge of finance systems & processes and ability to create cost saving or improve processes.

1. The profile confirms the candidate's qualified status, gives an outline of areas of expertise and the types & size of organisations worked for.

2. The core skills section highlights skills that are valued by finance teams such as finance systems & controls, asset management and internal auditing.

These bullet points jump out at the reader upon opening the CV - instantly showing the candidate's suitability for accounting roles.

3. Role descriptions start by outlining the role and organisation, who the candidate reports to and benchmark figures such as budget managed and number of people managed etc.

Responsibilities show exactly which financial processes have been managed/implemented and how they have improved processes or saved money for the company. They also show colleagues, stakeholders and external parties that the candidate liaises with.

Key achievements that show impressive amounts of money saved for the firm are a great way to show quantifiable value to employers and really make the CV stand out.

4. Education and professional memberships are often important in financial roles as many positions require qualifications for companies to abide by laws and regulations - so they are made bold and clear.

5. Accounting and finance IT system knowledge is highlighted as employers will have their own systems and need to know whether candidates can use them or not.

Is this an effective Graduate/Junior CV?

The main challenge that junior candidates coming straight from school, college or university face, is that they often lack relevant work experience.

However, this can be addressed by placing more focus on non-work related experience such as education, personal projects, volunteering etc. and ensuring the content is tailored towards the jobs you are applying for.

This candidate is a music graduate, applying for roles in the music-management space, but they have no paid employment experience in the profession.

You can also check out our guides on writing an effective graduate CV or school leaver CV.

1. The profile or personal statement focuses on the candidate's academic achievements and extra-curricular activities as they are all music industry related.

It doesn't mention any of the candidate's paid employment as none of it is relevant to music management.

2. The core skills section again focuses on academic achievements such as the degree in music management and skills that have been learnt outside of work, such as instrument playing and music production software.

An extra section called "Ongoing Musical Pursuits" has been added to show recruiters that the candidate is actively involved in the music industry, even though their current full-time job may not be music oriented.

This stops employers being put off by the candidate's current irrelevant role and allows them to showcase more of their music experience to create a good first impression.

3. Role descriptions are kept brief as music industry recruiters will not be interested in the candidate's part-time retail sales roles.

Roles are still well structured and written to ensure the CV remains professional throughout.

4. Education sections for junior candidates needs to be detailed in order to demonstrate skills and knowledge that will not yet have been gained through work experience.

This candidate details relevant personal music projects, music production software and shows practical skills that could be applied in the workplace.

5. Interests are not often necessary for experienced workers, but junior candidates can use them to showcase hobbies and interests that are related to their chosen profession.

Here the candidate backs up their technical skills and passion for music by writing about relevant musical pursuits to finalise the perfect CV.

Is this an effective IT CV?

The key to an interview winning IT CV, is to blend your technical knowledge with straight-forward business language, so that your CV will impress both technical and non-technical people alike.

An IT CV needs to contain all of the important technical terms that IT specialists will look for, but also be written in a way that can be understood by non-IT staff like recruiters and non-IT hiring managers.

1. The profile for this IT support candidate gives a summary of their IT knowledge with the type and size of companies they have experience working for. It also explains how their work supports the running of their employer's business to demonstrate their value.

2. The core skills section highlights important qualifications that recruiters will be scanning for such as CCNA and ITIL, whilst also including core duties that will be expected of IT support staff such as troubleshooting and SLAs.

If you have lots of qualifications and technical skills then you can swap these round when applying for different roles to ensure that you are highlighting the most relevant knowledge to employers for each vacancy.

3. Role descriptions start with an outline that explains where the candidate sits within the business, the type of support they provide and amount of users they are responsible for.

Responsibilities go into details around daily activities such as hardware installation and user support whilst being sure to include as many technologies as possible in your

CV, to show employers the systems and hardware the candidate is capable of working with.

Key Achievements are nicely quantified by including numbers of staff moved during relocation and percentage of issues dealt with inside SLA time frames.

4. Education sections for IT candidates can tend to be a bit larger than other sectors due to the large amounts of qualifications required to work with certain systems. Be sure to include all of your relevant qualifications to ensure that your CV will be found in relevant recruiter searches.

The most important qualifications should be repeated in your profile and/or core skills section. You can also add a Technical Skills section to reinforce some of your more generic skills that aren't limited to particular makes/models.

Is this an effective Management CV?

The overall goal of a management CV is to show recruiters that you are able to lead teams in an efficient way that is beneficial to the business.

These benefits will differ depending on your industry, but usually include objectives like generating revenue, managing & improving operations, saving costs and serving client needs.

1. The profile for this Estate Management candidate outlines the industry he operates in and includes lots of

important management terms like budget management, operations and team leadership

2. The core skills section includes important factors that employers will look for when recruiting somebody to manage a part of their business; including example figures of budgets managed and client relationships.

3. Role descriptions start by outlining important facts such as, number of people managed and type of clients served, as well as the overall goal of the candidate's management role.

Responsibilities detail day-to-day tasks, showing how they impact customers and the business as a whole. In management CVs, it's important to show how you can lead teams and organise individuals to achieve common goals and keep clients happy.

Key Achievements show solid quantifiable facts that impact the business such as increase in revenues and a decrease in customer complaints.

Is this an effective Marketing CV?

The function of marketing within any business is to drive leads to a website or physical shop, in order for them to be converted into customers.

So your marketing CV should explain how your skills and actions are used within marketing campaigns, and how you've helped the business to win new customers.

Marketing is hugely focused around results, so your CV should feature lots of facts and figures to prove the value that you've added.

1. The profile for this candidate highlights her specialism in digital marketing and gives an overview of the types of campaigns she has run for previous employers and the results she has achieved.

Essentially the profile explains how the candidate can help businesses to increase their customer base and demonstrates her value to potential employers.

2. The core skills section highlights the marketing tactics she uses in her campaigns to give recruiters a quick snapshot of her marketing skill set.

This includes important digital marketing terminology such as SEO and Social Media Marketing.

3. Role descriptions start with an outline of where the candidate sits within the business and what the overall goal of the role is.

Responsibilities delve into the detail of her campaigns, showing what tactics are engaged, who she interacts with and technologies and methods used to achieve marketing goals.

The key achievement sections give an excellent summary of a recent marketing campaign with a good amount of figures to quantify her success such as number of new customers gained and revenue generated.

4. This particular candidate has no formal marketing qualifications so she has kept her education section very brief.

Is this an effective Project Manager CV?

Project managers are mostly employed to oversee one or more large transitions that drive some form of improvement within an organisation.

Whether it's an office relocation, or installation of a new IT system, your project management CV needs to show that you are capable of taking an employer from A to B in an efficient and timely manner.

1. The profile gives an overview of the type of projects that the candidate manages (IT infrastructure) and gives a rough idea of the types of firms he usually works for and the value of an average project he would lead.

This information gives recruiters an instant indication of the companies and projects this candidate is suited for.

2. The core skills section goes into a bit moire detail around the candidate's technical skills, such as web conferencing and instant messaging, as well as recognised project management qualifications like Prince2.

These are the type of attributes that project management recruiters will have been briefed to look for, so it pays to highlight them.

3. Role descriptions start with a high level overview of the project to show readers the size and scale of the project as well as where the candidate sits in the hierarchy.

Responsibilities delve into the detail of daily/weekly tasks such as planning, reporting and leading workshops. It's important to show interaction with colleagues and stakeholders as well as showing how actions continually driving the project forward.

Key achievements round up some impressive figures from the project such as money and time saved on completion.

4. Due to the nature of project management, candidates will sometimes have worked for a large number of different employers over their career,(especially contractors) so older roles can be organised into list format to save space.

5. The education section only includes relevant project management and technical qualifications because that is all recruiters will want to see - the candidate can afford to leave out traditional education such as A levels, to save space if need be.

Is this an effective Sales CV?

Sales staff are expected to generate income for businesses by consistently closing sales, therefore your sales CV needs to prove that you can do this.

Sales is a results driven profession with a huge focus on results and figures, so employers will expect to see this reflected in your CV

1. The profile gives an overview of the candidate's sales skills such as account management, sales growth and relationship management; as well as showcasing product and service knowledge which is very important in sales roles.

2. The core skills section provides a good mix of sales skills and product knowledge in order to give a quick snapshot of relevant attributes to recruiters. This makes the CV much more likely to pass the initial scan.

3. Role descriptions start with an outline that shows the candidate's position in the business and which area she is responsible for driving sales in.

Responsibilities show the steps taken to achieve sales such as lead generation, networking and earning referrals. The candidate also showcases more in-depth product knowledge and details levels of customer and colleague interaction.

Quantifiable key achievements are crucial to a sales CV, so this candidate has included revenue generated, number of new customers acquired and increase in portfolio size.

4. Sales teams like to employ competitive individuals so this candidate has included some industry awards to showcase here abilities in that area.

10 STEPS TO A SUCCESSFUL CV

Writing a good CV can be one of the toughest challenges of job hunting. Most employers spend just a few seconds scanning each CV before sticking it in the 'Yes' or 'No' pile. Harsh.

But never fear! We've compiled our Top 10 hints on how to show the world 'this is me!' and get that all-important interview.

1. Keep it real!

Usually a CV should be no more than two pages – and that's two pages of A4 paper! Employers spend, on average, just 8 seconds looking at any one CV, and a surefire way of landing yourself on the no pile is to send them your entire life story. Keep it punchy, to the point, and save those niggly little details for the interview.

If you want examples then check out our free CV templates.

2. Tailor it

We've all done it. Whizzed the same CV out to lots of employers to save time... Stop! Take the time to change your CV for each role that you apply for. Research the company and use the job advert to work out EXACTLY what skills you should point out to them. They will appreciate the obvious effort.

3. Include a personal statement

Don't just assume an employer will see how your experience relates to their job. Instead, use a short personal statement to explain why you are the best person for the job. This should be reflected in your cover letter as well see our tips to the perfect cover letter

4. Don't leave gaps.

We are a cynical bunch and leaving obvious gaps on your CV immediately makes employers suspicious – and they won't give you the benefit of the doubt. If you've been out of work it can be a worry but just put a positive spin on it. Did you do a course, volunteer work or develop soft skills such as communication, teamwork or project management? If so, shout about it!

For more information, check out our CV template for the currently unemployed.

5. Keep it current

You should keep your CV up-to-date whether you're looking for a job or not. Every time something significant occurs in your career, record it so you don't later forget something that could be important.

6. The error of your ways

Employers DO look for mistakes on CVs and if they find them, it makes you look really bad. David Hipkin, head of recruitment and resourcing at Reed Business Information, warns, 'With most employers experiencing massive volumes of applicants right now, giving them the excuse to dismiss your application because of avoidable errors is not going to help you secure an interview.' If you're unsure then use a spellchecker and ask someone else to double-check what you've written. And don't ignore the most common CV mistakes

7. Tell the truth

Everyone lies on their CV, right? NO! Stop! Blatant lies on your CV can land you in a whole heap of trouble when it comes to employers checking your background and references. The last thing you want is to start work and then lose your new job for lying. You also may get caught out at the interview stage when you suddenly can't answer questions on what you claim to know. And that can be VERY awkward!

8. The maths

This may sound dull but by backing up your achievements with numbers it makes selling yourself much easier. When writing your work history, don't just say that you increased sales; tell them you increased sales by 70% over a six month period. Get it? Big numbers are especially good (although don't forget point 7 of our list!).

9. Make it look good

We live in a world where image is everything, and that also goes for your CV. Take some time to pretty it up... Use bullet points and keep sentences short. Use the graphic design trick of leaving plenty of white space around text and between categories to make the layout easy on the eye. Alternatively, get creative with your job application!

10. Make it keyword friendly

If you've uploaded your CV to a job site so recruiters can find you, keywords are very important. Job titles and job buzzwords will help a search engine pick out your CV from the pile. Confused? Don't be. A marketing candidate might mention SEO (Search Engine Optimization), direct marketing and digital marketing among their experience and skills, for example... If you're not sure, have a search online and see what words are commonly mentioned when you input your job title.

CONCLUSION

A CV is the most flexible and convenient way to make applications. It conveys your personal details in the way that presents you in the best possible light. Your CV, short for curriculum vitae, is a personal marketing document used to sell yourself to prospective employers. It should tell them about you, your professional history and your skills, abilities and achievements. When it comes to job hunting, your CV is paramount. Get it right, and you'll have an interview in no time, but get it wrong, and you may face rejection after rejection. Every CV is different as you want to show why your set of skills makes you suitable for the position you're applying for at that moment, but all follow a similar structure. Ultimately, it should highlight why you're the best person for the job.

www.ingramcontent.com/pod-product-compliance
Lightning Source LLC
Chambersburg PA
CBHW030510220526
45464CB00006B/2730